W9-BDL-301

VIVA!
LATINO CELEBRATIONS

CELEBRATING
CHRISTMAS!

MARISA ORGULLO

PowerKiDS press.

New York

Published in 2019 by The Rosen Publishing Group, Inc.
29 East 21st Street, New York, NY 10010

Copyright © 2019 by The Rosen Publishing Group, Inc.

All rights reserved. No part of this book may be reproduced in any form without permission in writing from the publisher, except by a reviewer.

First Edition

Editor: Brianna Battista
Book Design: Reann Nye

Photo Credits: Cover (child) Anton Bogodvid/Shutterstock.com; cover (background) Peter Donaldson/Alamy.com; p. 5 Natali99/Shutterstock.com; p. 7 Annie Wells/Getty Images; p. 9 Fer Gregory/Shutterstock.com; p. 11 GoneWithTheWind/Shutterstock.com; p. 13 sumikophoto/Shutterstock.com; p. 15 Carolina Arroyo/Shutterstock.com; p. 17 GUILLERMO LEGARIA/AFP/Getty Images; p. 19 Jose Luis Pelaez Inc/ Blend Images/Getty Images; p. 21 Playa del Carmen/Shutterstock.com; p. 22 Sofiaworld/Shutterstock.com.

Library of Congress Cataloging-in-Publication Data

Names: Orgullo, Marisa, author.
Title: Celebrating Christmas! / Marisa Orgullo.
Description: New York : PowerKids Press, [2019] | Series: Viva! Latino
   celebrations | Includes index.
Identifiers: LCCN 2018025603| ISBN 9781538342107 (Library bound) | ISBN
   9781538342084 (Paperback) | ISBN 9781538342091 (6 pack)
Subjects: LCSH: Christmas–Latin America–Juvenile literature. |
   Christmas–Mexico–Juvenile literature. | Latin America–Social life and
   customs–Juvenile literature. | Mexico–Social life and customs–Juvenile
   literature.
Classification: LCC GT4987.155 .O74 2019 | DDC 394.2663098–dc23
LC record available at https://lccn.loc.gov/2018025603

Manufactured in the United States of America

CPSIA Compliance Information: Batch Batch #CWPK19: For Further Information contact Rosen Publishing, New York, New York at 1-800-237-9932

CONTENTS

A Special Season 4

The Story of Las Posadas 8

Honoring the
Three Wise Men 16

Glossary. 23

Index 24

Websites 24

A Special Season

December is a busy month for many Latin American people! They're preparing to **celebrate** Christmas, or the day when **Christians** believe that Jesus was born. In Latin America, the Christmas season is called la Navidad (nah-vee-THAHD). It's a season when many people spend time with their families in a special and joyful way.

Lights are a big part of la Navidad. Shown here is a big lit-up Christmas tree in Bogotá, Colombia.

5

During la Navidad, Mexicans and many other Latinos take part in a nine-day celebration called Las Posadas (poh-SAH-thahs). It begins December 16 and ends December 24. Las Posadas honors Joseph and Mary's search for a place for Jesus to be born. Christians believe that they had to go from place to place until they found safety in a **stable**.

Joseph and Mary were looking for a place to stay in Bethlehem because Mary was ready to have the baby.

The Story of Las Posadas

During Las Posadas, children and adults remember this special story. They play the parts of Mary and Joseph as they seek a room in a posada, or **inn**. Joseph and Mary knock on doors while singing. Each night, an innkeeper finally welcomes them. Inside, a party waits. Everyone sings and eats, and children hit a **piñata**. Many people are dressed in silver and gold.

Las Posadas is a celebration full of music and singing.

Many Latinos make crafts during la Navidad. One craft that many families like to build is a *nacimiento* (nah-sih-mee-EN-toh), or a model of the stable in which Jesus was born. They add figures of Mary and Joseph inside it. Then, children place the baby Jesus in his bed on *la Nochebuena* (NOH-chay BWAY-nah), or Christmas Eve. In English, a *nacimiento* is called a nativity scene.

The *nacimiento* has figures of Mary, Joseph, and baby Jesus inside. Sometimes it includes other figures too, such as sheep from the stable!

11

Christmas Eve is celebrated in different ways from country to country in Latin America. Many families go to church. Ecuador's people count down the minutes until midnight, the time that some people believe Jesus was born. Puerto Ricans and Dominicans sing songs. Many Latin American children open gifts. Most families share a big meal together.

This church is decorated with beautiful lights for la Navidad.

13

Many families celebrate on Christmas Day with a big feast! Families cook turkey, ham, and special **tamales**. Puerto Ricans eat *pasteles* (pahs-TEL-es), tamales cooked in banana leaves. Mexican children munch on cookies called *biscochitos* (bee-skoh-CHEE-tohs). Panamanians enjoy rice with pineapple. Sugared breads are common Christmas desserts throughout Latin America.

Tamales are a special food for la Navidad. To eat them, you unwrap the corn leaves from the outside.

Honoring the Three Wise Men

An important part of la Navidad comes after Christmas Day. *Los tres Reyes magos* (TREHS RAY-es MAH-gohs), or the Three Wise Men, have a story that's celebrated on January 6. The Three Wise Men are said to have been kings who brought gifts to the baby Jesus that day. On this holiday, many Latin Americans receive gifts. There are also colorful parades in the streets.

These teens are dressed up as the Three Wise Men for a parade in Bogotá, Colombia.

Many children in Puerto Rico start preparing for the holiday the night before the Three Wise Men come. They place boxes of grass under their beds on the night of January 5. They believe that this grass is for the Three Wise Men's camels to eat. When the children wake up in the morning, they may find presents where the grass once was!

Many children open gifts during la Navidad, though not all families celebrate this way.

19

Latin Americans bake special bread called *rosca de reyes* (ROH-skah DAY RAY-es), or bread of kings, for el Día (DEE-uh) de los tres Reyes. This bread is shaped like a ring and filled with dried fruits and nuts. Everyone enjoys a piece with cups of hot chocolate. Children sometimes make crowns to wear at the table to honor the kings.

In Mexico City, someone made a *rosca de reyes* that was a mile long! Over 200,000 people were able to try a piece.

La Navidad is a special time in Latin America. Many people take time to celebrate the birth of Jesus and to honor Joseph, Mary, and the Three Wise Men. Families and friends come together to share food and sing songs. Most importantly, people wish each other a *¡Feliz Navidad!* (fel-EES nah-vee-THAHD), or Merry Christmas!

GLOSSARY

celebrate: To honor an important moment by doing special things.

Christian: A person who believes in the teachings of Jesus Christ.

inn: A place where travelers can get food and a place to sleep.

piñata: A special container filled with candies. Children break the container with sticks.

stable: A building in which farm animals are kept and fed.

tamale: Cornmeal dough rolled with ground meat or beans and seasoning, wrapped in corn husks, and steamed.

INDEX

B
Bethlehem, 6
biscochitos, 14
Bogotá, 4, 16

C
Christians, 4, 6
Colombia, 4, 16

D
December, 4, 6
Dia de los tres Reyes, 20
Dominicans, 12

E
Ecuador, 12

J
Jesus, 4, 6, 10, 12, 16, 22
Joseph, 6, 8, 10, 22

L
la Nochebuena, 10
Las Posadas, 6, 8
lights, 4, 12
los tres Reyes magos, 16

M
Mary, 6, 8, 10, 22
Mexicans, 6, 14
Mexico City, 20
music, 8

N
nacimiento, 10

P
Panamanians, 14
pasteles, 14
Puerto Ricans, 12, 14
Puerto Rico, 18

R
rosca de reyes, 20

T
tamales, 14
Three Wise Men, 16, 18, 22

WEBSITES

Due to the changing nature of Internet links, PowerKids Press has developed an online list of websites related to the subject of this book. This site is updated regularly. Please use this link to access the list: www.powerkidslinks.com/lcila/christmas